"Joshua & Mommy's Crazy Book"

By: Joshua Josma & Mommy (Tasha Taylor)

"Table of Content"

- Chapter 1: Joshua & Mommy's Crazy Book….5
- Chapter 2: Joshua Knows about Guns…12
- Chapter 3: Never touch a weapon,

unless you know how to use it…25
- Chapter 4: More About Me…29
- Chapter 5: Pictures by Joshua Josma…55
- Biography…68

Chapter 1: "Joshua & Mommy's Crazy Book"

This was Joshua's birthday picture last year. We went to the Race Track in Orlando Florida.

My son has a heart for animals and loves to see that they are protected.

For Christmas Joshua
wants 2 Dalmatian
puppies

He also wants a
drivable toy car to
take to the park.

Joshua wants to become a Judge in Washington, D.C.

Joshua also wants to become a Millionaire!

Chapter 2:
"Joshua Knows About Guns"

I am Joshua

I am here today to tell you something about gun's, bombs and T.N.T's.

Some people watch TV,

and see some guns
and they think that if
they have a gun they
can rob a bank;

…but, I'm here to tell you that guns are not good,

…because people see some stuff and they wish they could do that, like rob a bank.

They see bad stuff in movies and bombs are dangerous too.

Never touch guns or grenade's too because they can explode…

…and you don't have enough time to throw it.

I will show you a lot of pictures when I'm finished talking…

…and I know you've seen some of the pictures that are on the book I just made.

This is the kind of stuff you should not be around.

Chapter 3:

"Never touch a weapon, unless you know how to use it."

Children at any age should not use weapons. I am Joshua's Mom and think that Fortnite should be

…banned from schools and children less than 15 years of age.

So, I guess this book
is not so crazy
Afterall…

Chapter 4:
More About Me…

I am a Christian and I
  love to go to Jesus.

My favorite story in the Bible is found in Proverbs chapter 5. It is about the "Ant and the Sluggard."

One thing that I enjoy
about this story is
how brave and

hardworking the ant is

… to take care of its family.

He works hard in the winter,

…just to make sure
that his family has
food to eat.

He is very small in size

...but through teamwork the ants end up having so much food...

that it last them
through the cold
winter.

This way they are
able to sleep and rest
during the cold
winter..

with a large supply of food.

On the other hand, the sluggard is lazy.

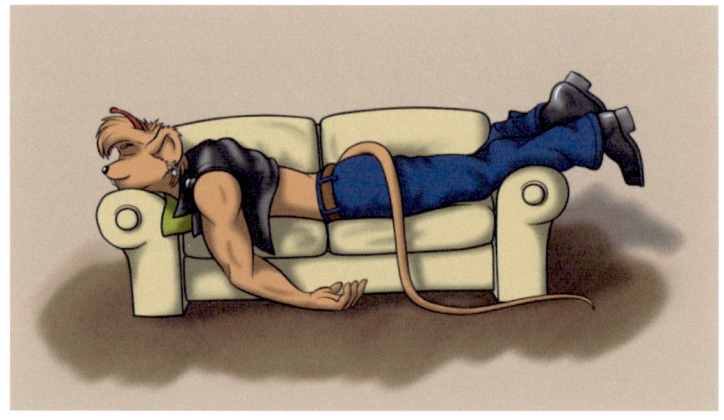

He sleeps all day and
waits until it's too late
to look for food.

During the winter its cold and there is frost everywhere. Most of all the trees

have no food on them.

The sluggard will starve to death

…if he doesn't get food.

So he goes around
and looks for the ants,

...because he suspects
that they would have
food in this season

…and ask for food.

However, the ant is so
small and the
sluggard so large.

Why would he need help from a tiny ant?

But, at the end of the sluggard ask the ant for food…

… and thankfully the
ant has a large supply.

It is important to store up in during times of plenty…

…so that if a drought comes you can have plenty saved up

… for your family!

Chapter 5:
Pictures by Joshua Josma

This is a ladybug who is in the rain. He is eating his food.

This is the Cross that Jesus died on for our sins. The cross is surrounded by stars that I call Angels.

This is a musical sign
that I made and it's
for crazy ...really
weird sign!

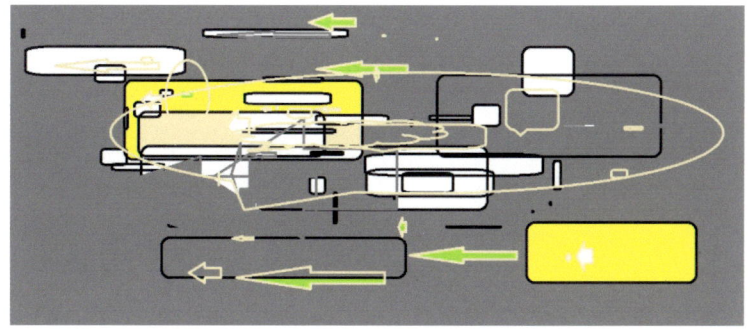

Did you ever see a green star like this? Or, a green shirt like this?

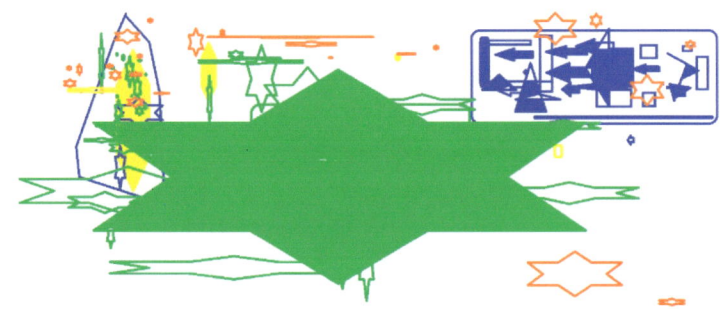

Why does this say AFC? Because, I forgot to put KFC… Ha, Ha, Ha….

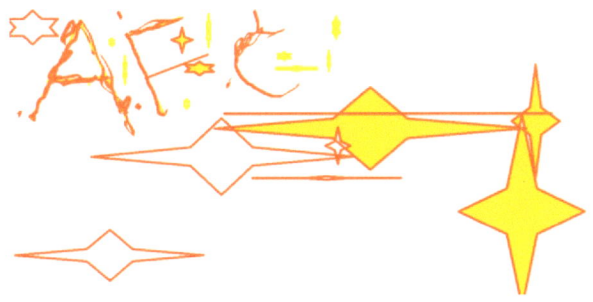

Have you heard that
your mind looks like a
dirty thing? Well this
is what it looks like,
right here!

Have you heard that science is a rocks that exploding on each other to create the universe. That's a bunch of crap!

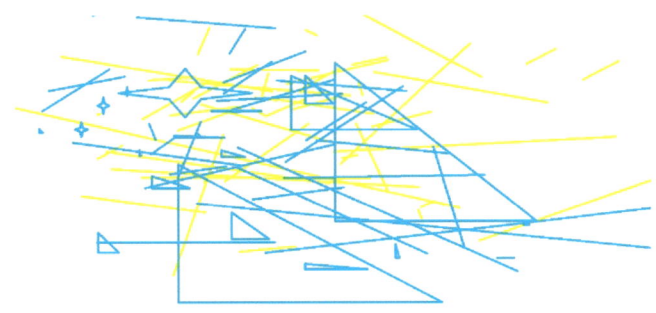

Who made this lovely creature? Definitely not rocks banging together. Ha, Ha, Ha,

Do you know picture signs have ovals, blocks, and people in them. This is my latest creation.

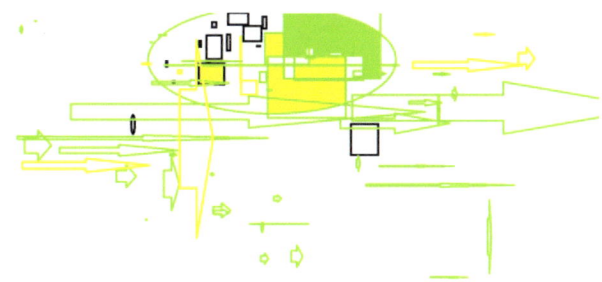

Do you know that people can jump on a sign and hurt themselves getting to their next destination?

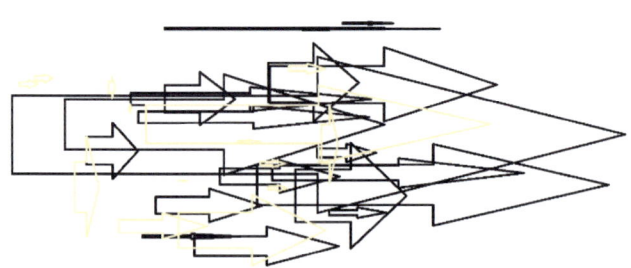

This is the last exhibit of my art gallery for you today…But there's more. My Moms going to talk to you a little bit.

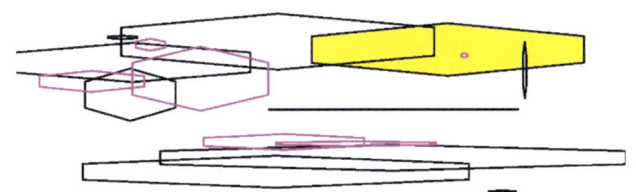

"Biograph of Joshua"

Joshua was born on March 12, 2010 to Tasha & Michelet.

They were married, divorced when Joshua was about 4 years old.

Now Joshua is 9 years old and he loves pets,

drawing,

Pictures,

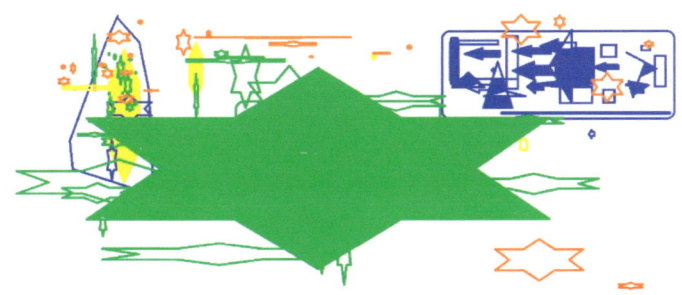

Like this,

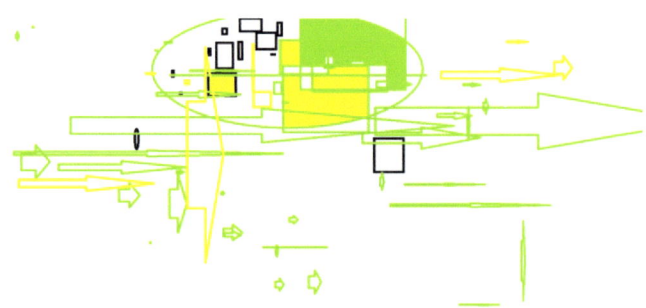

And this,

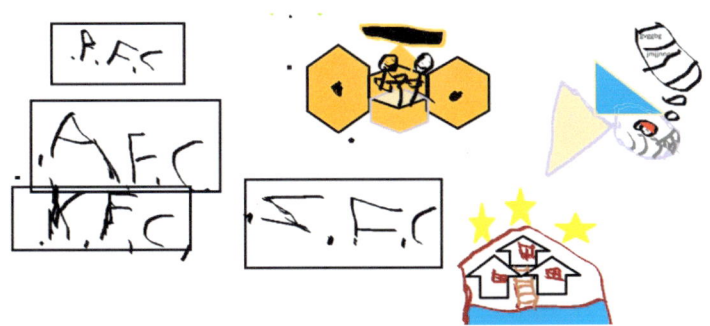

Like this one,

And this one,

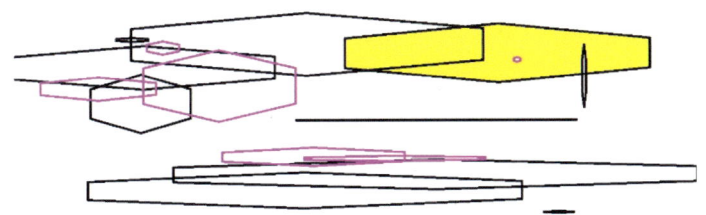

And this too,

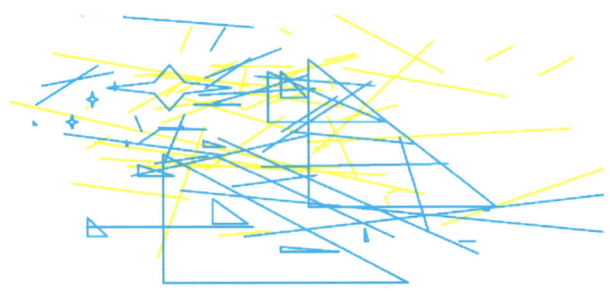

And of course this
one,

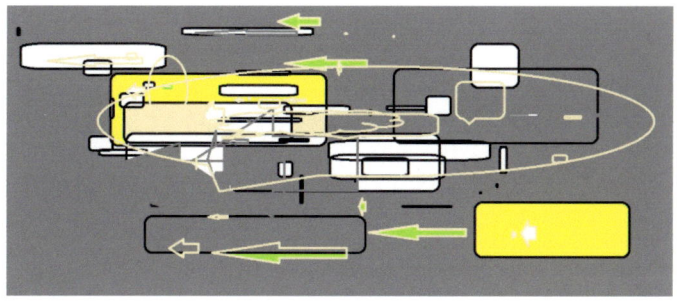

And oh don't forget
this one,

And this one too…

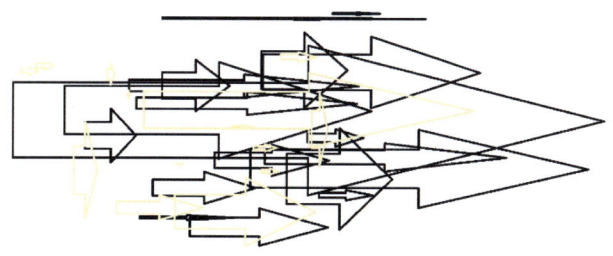

…making color rocks
and more.

This is his first
published book

Joshua loves to eat chicken

Cheese Pizza…

Macaroni & Cheese…

Jamaican Food,

And like this…

And not to forget like this…

And this…

And also this,

…And this.

Joshua also likes to drink Lemonade,

Gatorade…

Sprite soda…

And of course, how can I forget, doughnuts…

Candy

Joshua loves to skate….

And he likes the
scooter…

And now he is the author of his first book called, "Joshua & Mommy's Crazy Book."

And co-Author Mommy

The End.

Made in the USA
Columbia, SC
15 March 2025

54949814R00058